Investigate

Water

Charlotte Guillain

Heinemann Library
Chicago, Illinois

2008 Heinemann Library
a division of Pearson Inc.
Chicago, Illinois

Customer Service 888-454-2279
Visit our website at www.heinemannraintree.com

Designed by Joanna Hinton-Malivoire Victoria Bevan, and Hart McLeod
Printed in China by Leo Paper Group

12 11 10 09 08
10 9 8 7 6 5 4 3 2 1

The Library of Congress has cataloged the first edition as follows:
Guillain, Charlotte.
  Water / Charlotte Guillain.
    p. cm. -- (Investigate)
  Includes bibliographical references and index.
  ISBN 978-1-4329-1393-9 (hc) -- ISBN 978-1-4329-1409-7 (pb) 1. Water--Juvenile literature. I. Title.
  GB662.3.G85 2008
  551.48--dc22

                              2008006814

Acknowledgments
The publishers would like to thank the following for permission to reproduce photographs: ©Alamy pp. **5** (Stock Connection Distribution), **16**, **30** (D. Hurst), **19** (Digital Archive Japan); ©Corbis pp. **6** (Arctic-Images), **6** (Scot Smith), **13** (Matt Sullivan/Reuters), **15** (David Muench); ©Getty Images pp. **8** (PhotoDisc), **10** (Image Bank), **18** (Photonica), **20** (Steve Casmiro/Riser), **22** (Taxi), **23**, **28** (Stone), **26**, **29**, **30** (Riser), **27** (Iconica); ©Istockphoto pp. **7** (Kent Metschan), **30** (Plainview); ©Masterfile p. **14** (Daniel Barillot); ©Photolibrary p. **4** (OSF); ©Science Photo Library pp. **7** (Cordelia Molloy), **24** (Mike Boyatt/Agstockusa), **25** (Cape Grim B.A.P.S./Simon Fraser); ©Tips Images p. **11** (Raymond Forbes).

Cover photograph reproduced with permission of ©Getty Images (Norbert Wu/Science Faction).

Every effort has been made to contact copyright holders of any material reproduced in this book.
Any omissions will be rectified in subsequent printings if notice is given to the publisher.

Contents

Some words are shown in bold, **like this**. You can find out what they mean by looking in the glossary.

Water for Life

Plants, animals, and people are living things.
All living things need water to live.

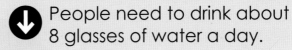 People need to drink about 8 glasses of water a day.

More than half your body is water. People need to drink water to stay healthy. People also need water to wash themselves and to grow plants for food.

Bodies of Water

Water is on Earth in bodies of water. There are different types of bodies of water.

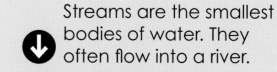

Streams are the smallest bodies of water. They often flow into a river.

Water bubbles up through mountain springs and flows into streams.

Rivers are large, flowing bodies of water. They move water in one direction.

Lakes are large bodies of water with land all around them. Rivers can flow into lakes.

Q What are the largest bodies of water?

7

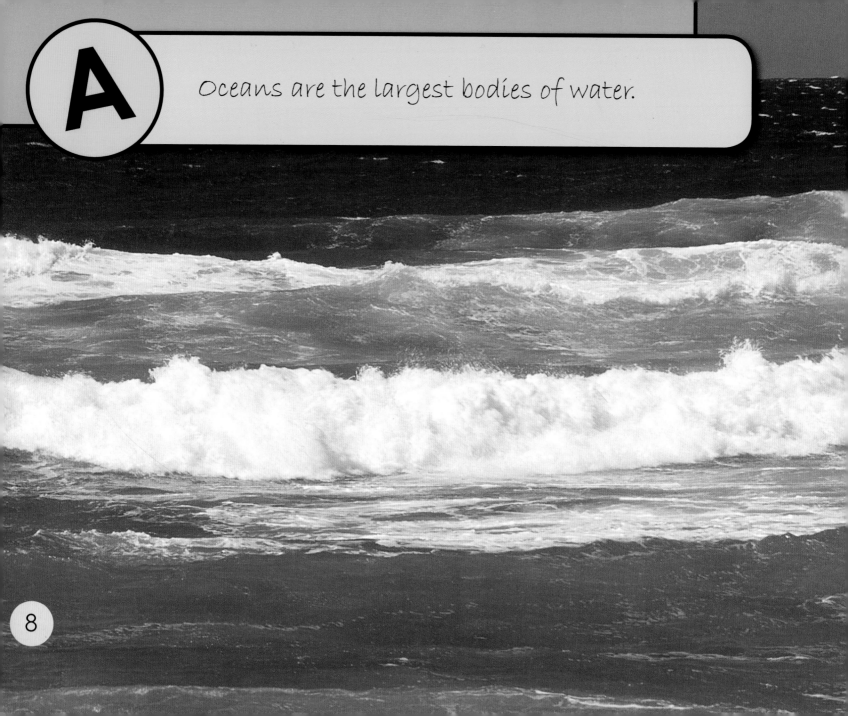

A Oceans are the largest bodies of water.

8

This map shows the five oceans of the world.

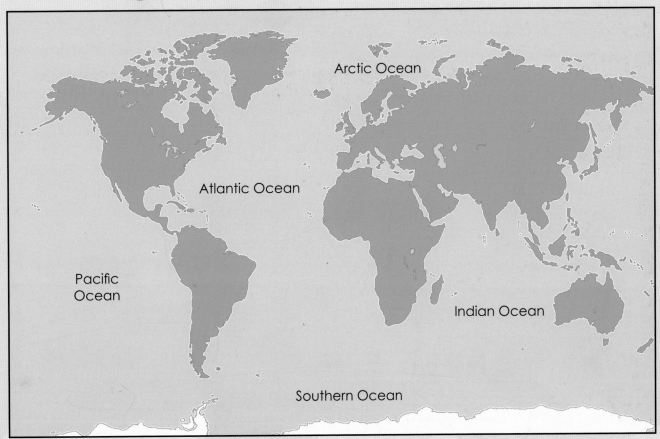

OCEAN FACTS

➡ The Pacific Ocean is the largest ocean.

➡ Almost all of the water on Earth is salt water.
It is found in the oceans.

9

Changing Water

Most of the water in oceans is **liquid**. The water we drink and wash with is liquid. Rainwater is liquid.

Q What happens when water gets very cold?

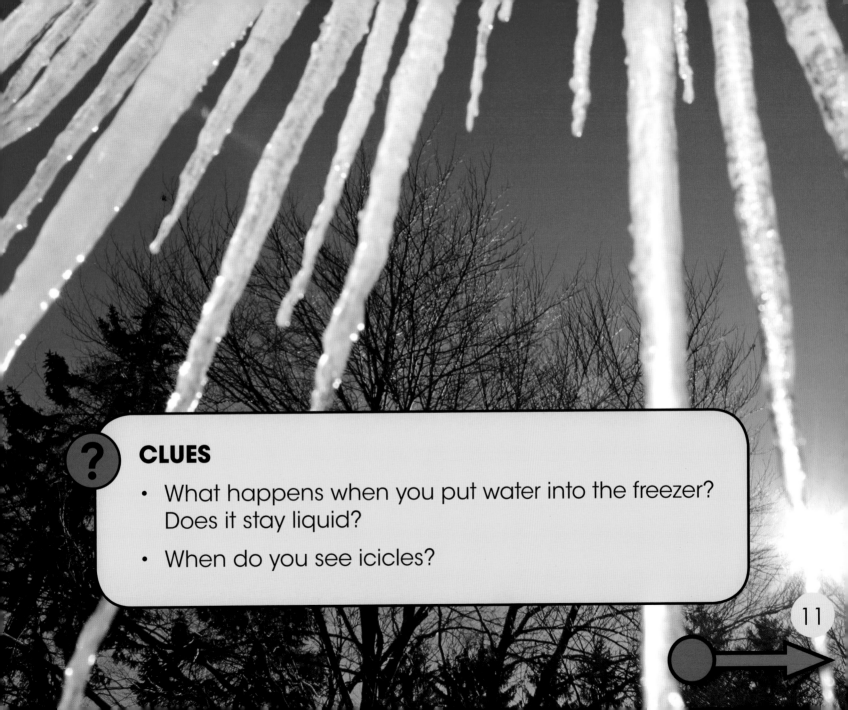

CLUES

- What happens when you put water into the freezer? Does it stay liquid?

- When do you see icicles?

A

When water gets very cold it **freezes**. Frozen water is **solid**.

Water freezes when the **temperature** is below 32°F (0°C). A **thermometer** measures the temperature.

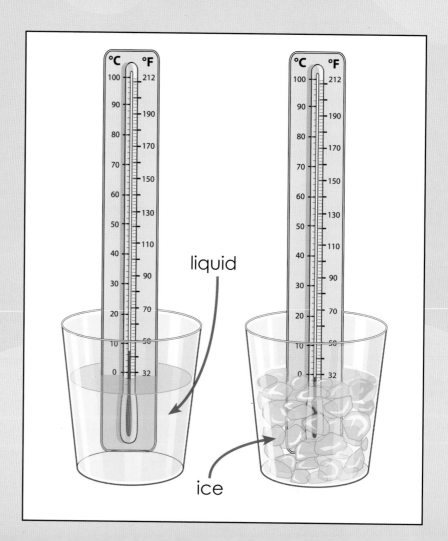

liquid

ice

Frozen water is called ice. Ice can be used to:

➠ keep food fresh

➠ keep drinks cold

➠ play sports such as skating and ice hockey

➠ make **sculptures**

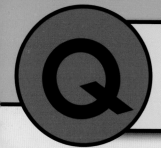

Q What happens when water gets warm?

15

? **CLUES**

- What do you see when a pot of water boils?

- What happens to a puddle when the sun shines?

When water gets warm, it evaporates and becomes **water vapor**. When water gets very hot, it boils and becomes steam.

Water boils when the temperature is 212°F (100°C).
When water boils it turns from a liquid into a gas.
When water turns into a gas it **evaporates**. The water
vapor rises into the air.

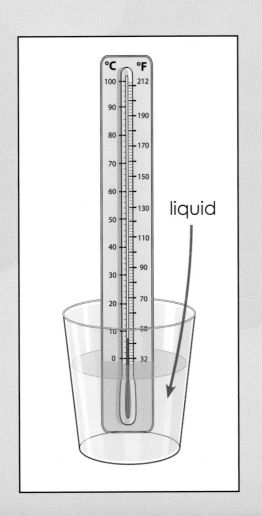

liquid

steam

17

The Water Cycle

What happens when the sun shines on a lake?

CLUES

- Does the sun make the water warmer or colder?

- What happens to water when it gets warm?

A

When the sun shines on a lake, the water **evaporates**. The water becomes **water vapor** and rises into the air.

 Water vapor in the air makes clouds in the sky.

There are different types of clouds, including:

- → Cumulus clouds. These look puffy. We can see these clouds on a sunny day. It might rain when there are cumulus clouds.

- → Cirrus clouds. These look thin and wispy. They are found very high in the sky. It doesn't rain when there are only cirrus clouds in the sky.

- → Stratus clouds. These stretch out in flat layers. There could be rain when there are stratus clouds.

- → Cumulonimbus clouds. These are very large. There may be a storm where there are cumulonimbus clouds.

21

Q When the **temperature** cools, what happens to the clouds?

22

CLUE

- What happens when steam from a shower touches a cold mirror?

When the temperature cools, water vapor turns to **liquid**. Steam turns to liquid when it hits a cold window or mirror. This is called **condensation**. When water vapor in a cloud cools, it rains. This is also called condensation.

People can use a **rain gauge** to measure how much rain has fallen. The rain gauge catches rainwater so people can measure it.

When it rains, the water falls back into rivers, lakes, and oceans. Water also falls on to the soil and goes into the ground.

Plants get water from the soil through their roots. Plants need water and sunlight to live and grow.

27

People can also get water from under the ground. Many people get their water from underground wells. Other people get their water from rivers and lakes. The water travels through pipes to taps in people's houses.

The water we use has travelled a long way. It has gone from bodies of water to clouds and back again as rain. Plants and animals can only live on Earth because of water. Water is very important in our lives so we must not waste a tiny drop.

Checklist

Living things such as plants, animals, and people need water.

Water can be:

liquid

solid

gas

Bodies of water include:

➡ streams
➡ rivers
➡ lakes
➡ oceans

Glossary

condensation when water vapor cools and turns back into a liquid

evaporate when liquid heats up and turns into a gas

freeze when a liquid cools and turns into a solid

gas substance like air that completely fills any container in which it is kept and has no shape of its own

liquid something that flows, such as water and oil

rain gauge a tool for measuring how much rain has fallen

sculpture a statue or carving

solid something which has a definite shape. Ice, wood, and stone are all solid.

temperature how hot or cold something is

thermometer a tool for measuring the temperature

water vapor water in the form of gas. Steam is water vapor.

Index